Exploring Space Science

MW00897548

Daily Science Workbook

for kids in Grades 4-5 To Master the Subject and Ace the Tests!

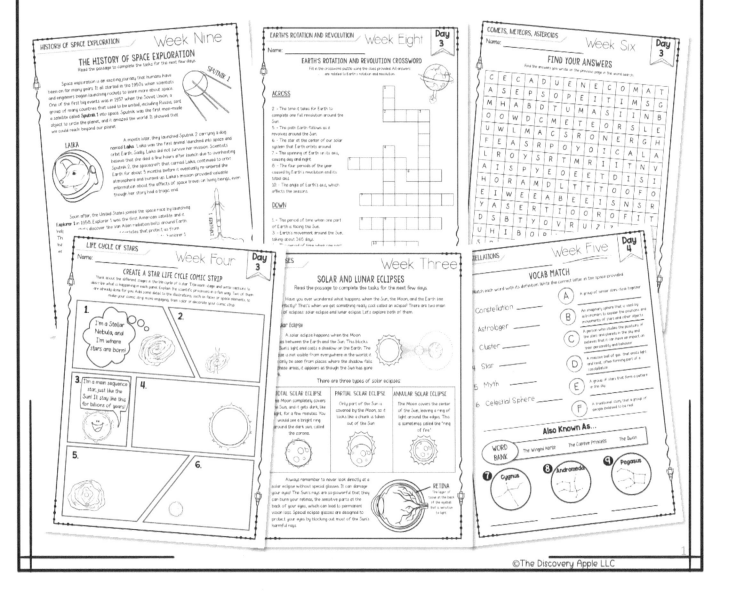

Written by Fatema Ghazi
Illustrations by Mariam Ghazi

Contact the author:
Fatema@thediscoveryapple.com

Workbook Highlights

WEEKLY TOPICS

Each week focuses on a different science topic, such as the planets, moon phases, constellations, asteroids, comets, stars, etc.

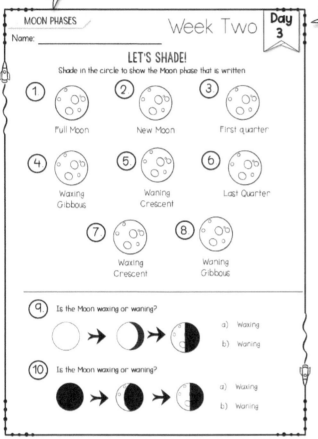

DAILY WORKSHEETS

Each topic consists of five worksheets, one for each weekday.

VARIETY OF ACTIVITIES

Each topic is explored through different types of activities:

- Reading Comprehension: Students read passages related to the topic and answer questions to demonstrate their understanding.
- Vocabulary: Activities focus on building and reinforcing vocabulary related to the topic, helping students grasp important scientific terms and concepts.
- Labeling Diagrams: Students practice identifying and labeling parts of diagrams or illustrations related to the topic, enhancing their understanding of its components.
- Critical Thinking Writing Response: Students are prompted to think critically about the topic and express their ideas through writing. These prompts encourage them to analyze, evaluate, and reflect on what they've learned, fostering higher-order thinking skills and creativity.

REVIEW AND REINFORCEMENT

Can be used as review and reinforcement of key concepts. You can use it alongside their regular science curriculum to deepen their understanding of daily space science topics.

FLEXIBLE USE

Can be used in various ways, such as for homework assignments, independent study, or as part of a classroom lesson. It can also serve as a tool for assessment and progress tracking.

TABLE OF CONTENTS

THIS BOOK BELONGS TO:

_____

MY SCIENCE GOALS AND INTERESTS

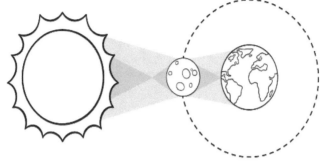

Write down at least three things you hope to learn more about in science. You can also write down any questions you have about the world around you that you hope to find answers to.

1. _____

_____

2. _____

_____

_____

3. _____

_____

Do you have any specific topics you're excited to learn about? What are they? Share your interests here:

_____

_____

_____

_____

_____

_____

Week One

The PLANETS

Jupiter is so big that you could fit over 1,300 Earths inside it—making it the largest planet in our solar system!

Week One

Read the passage to complete the tasks for the next few days.

EXPLORING THE PLANETS

We have 8 planets in our solar system orbiting, or circling, the Sun.

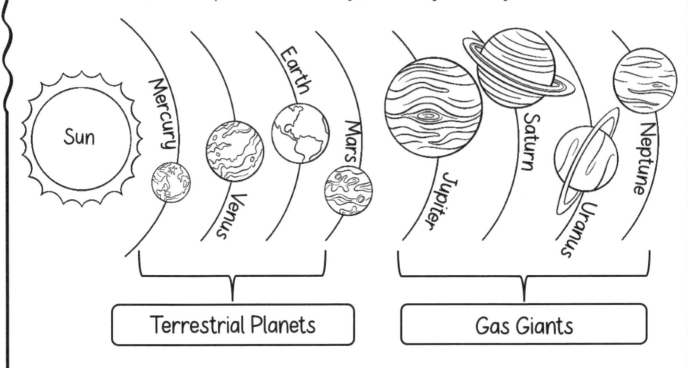

Terrestrial Planets

Gas Giants

THE TERRESTRIAL PLANETS

The terrestrial planets, also known as the rocky planets, are the four innermost planets of the solar system. They are made of rock and metal and have solid surfaces.

MERCURY

Mercury is the smallest planet and closest to the Sun. It has a very thin atmosphere, which means it can't retain heat. So, its surface experiences extreme temperatures, both hot and cold.

FUN FACT

A year on Mercury (one orbit around the Sun) takes just 88 Earth days!

VENUS

Venus is known as Earth's sister because it is almost identical in size, composition, gravity, and density. Unlike Earth, the atmosphere on Venus is mostly carbon dioxide, with clouds of sulfuric acid that trap heat, making it the hottest planet in the solar system. Venus also has volcanoes, mountains, and vast plateaus.

FUN FACT

Venus rotates very slowly and in the opposite direction to most planets, meaning a day on Venus is longer than a year!

Week One

EARTH

Earth is the third planet from the Sun and the only one known to support life. It is the only planet that has 21% oxygen which make life possible. It has a perfect mix of air, water, and land, making it a vibrant place full of plants, animals, and humans. Earth tilts on its axis, which gives us the seasons.

FUN FACT
29% of Earth is covered with land and 71 % is covered by water.

MARS

Mars is known as the Red Planet due to its reddish appearance, which comes from iron oxide (rust) on its surface. It has the tallest volcano and the deepest canyon in the solar system. Mars lacks oxygen, has lots of dust storms, and does not have water.

FUN FACT
Mars has two small moons, Phobos and Deimos.

THE GAS GIANTS

The gas giants are the four outermost planets. They are much larger than terrestrial planets and are made mostly of gases like hydrogen and helium.

JUPITER

Jupiter is the largest planet in our solar system. It has a Great Red Spot, which is a massive storm bigger than Earth. Jupiter spins around much faster than Earth, so day and night is every 9.84 hours rather than 24 hours! In fact, Jupiter is the fastest spinning planet in the solar system. Thick colorful clouds surrounding Jupiter are deadly poisonous gases mostly made of ammonia, crystals, and sulfur.

FUN FACT
Jupiter has at least 79 moons.

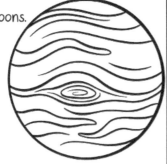

SATURN

Saturn is the second-largest planet in our solar system. It is a great ball of hydrogen and helium. Saturn is famous for its beautiful ring system, made up of ice and rock particles. It has at least 18 moons that orbit around the planet.

FUN FACT
Saturn's largest moon, Titan, is bigger than the planet Mercury and has a thick atmosphere.

Week One

URANUS

Uranus is the 7th planet from the Sun. It was the first planet discovered by a telescope. Uranus is unique because it rotates on its side, making its axis nearly horizontal. It has a faint ring system and is known for its blue-green color due to methane in its atmosphere.

FUN FACT

Uranus has 27 known moons, named after characters from the works of Shakespeare and Alexander Pope.

NEPTUNE

Neptune is the farthest planet from the Sun and is known for its deep blue color. It has strong winds and storms, including the Great Dark Spot, similar to Jupiter's Great Red Spot. In fact, Neptune has the windiest weather in the solar system. Wind speeds on Neptune can reach up to 1,500 miles per hour, which is faster than the speed of sound on Earth.

FUN FACT

Neptune's moon Triton is one of the coldest places in our solar system and has geysers that spew nitrogen gas.

Name: _____

Week One

WHICH PLANET AM I?

After reading and learning all about the fascinating planets in our solar system, can you identify which planet is being described? Draw a line from each description to the correct planet.

1 I was the first planet discovered by a telescope and I rotate on my side. Who am I?

2 I am the smallest planet in our solar system and I am the closest planet to the Sun. Who am I?

3 71% of my surface is covered with water and I have one moon. Who am I?

4 I am the second largest planet and I am famous for my beautiful rings, made up of ice and rock. Who am I?

5 I am the largest and the fastest spinning planet in the solar system. Who am I?

6 I am known as the Red Planet and I have the tallest volcano in the solar system. Who am I?

7 I am the farthest planet in our solar system and I have the windiest weather. Who am I?

8 I am the hottest planet and I spin backwards compared to most planets. Who am I?

JUPITER

VENUS

URANUS

NEPTUNE

SATURN

EARTH

MERCURY

MARS

Week One

Name: _____

List the planets in the correct order and indicate whether each one is a Terrestrial planet or a Gas Giant on the line next to it. Write 'Terrestrial' or 'Gas Giant' on the line next to each one.

WORD BANK

Mars   Jupiter   Venus   Uranus
   Neptune   Mercury   Saturn   Earth

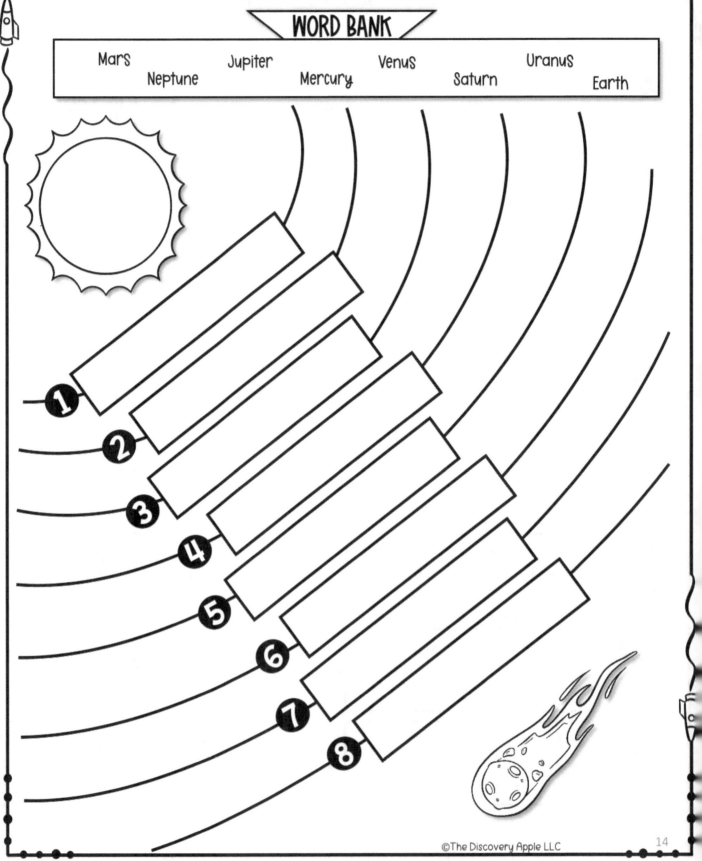

14

Name: _____

EXPLORING THE PLANETS

After learning about the planets, answer the following questions.

1. What is unique about Uranus's rotation?

   a) It rotates very quickly
   b) It rotates the opposite direction of most planets
   c) It rotates on its side
   d) It rotates very slowly

2. Which planet is known for having the Great Red Spot?

   a) Mars
   b) Jupiter
   c) Saturn
   d) Neptune

3. What makes Venus the hottest planet in our solar system?

   a) Its closeness to the Sun
   b) Its thick, toxic atmosphere
   c) Its fast rotation
   d) Its large number of volcanoes

4. Which planet has a moon named Triton?

   a) Neptune
   b) Saturn
   c) Jupiter
   d) Mars

5. True or False: (If your answer is false, rewrite the answer to make it true)
   Earth is farther from the Sun than Mars.

6. What are the key differences between terrestrial planets and gas giants?

7. Choose one planet and explain what makes it unique.

Name: _____

Vocab Match

Match each word with its definition. Write the correct letter in the space provided.

1. Terrestrial Planets _____

2. Gas Giants _____

3. Orbit _____

4. Atmosphere _____

5. Gravity _____

6. Rotation _____

7. Revolution _____

8. Axis _____

9. Moons _____

10. Solar System _____

(A) An imaginary line that a planet spins around, causing day and night.
_____

(B) The path that a planet takes around the Sun.
_____

(C) Natural satellites that orbit planets.
_____

(D) Large Planets made mostly of gases, including Jupiter, Saturn, Uranus, and Neptune
_____

(E) The force that pulls objects towards the center of a planet
_____

(F) Planets that are rocky and close to the Sun, such as Mercury, Venus, Earth, and Mars
_____

(G) The movement of one object around another
_____

(H) The spinning of a planet on its axis.
_____

(I) The Sun and all the objects that orbit it, including planets, moons, asteroids, and comets.
_____

(J) The layer of gases surrounding a planet

If you were tasked with planning a mission to another planet, which planet would you choose and why?

Week Two

Moon

PHASES

The Moon's phases change as it orbits Earth, from a new moon that's completely dark to a full moon that lights up the night sky like a giant, glowing lantern!

PHASES OF THE MOON

Read the passage to complete the tasks for the next few days.

As the Moon orbits Earth, the Sun lights up different parts of it, making it seem as if the Moon is changing shape. The Moon's shape never changes. We are only able to see the Sun's light reflected off of the Moon's surface. The different shapes of the Moon that we see from Earth are called the **phases of the Moon.**

It takes the Moon a lunar month, or 29.5 days, to go through its eight different phases. When the bright part of the Moon is getting bigger, the Moon is '**waxing**' and when it is getting smaller, the Moon is '**waning**'.

During the **New Moon** phase, the Moon is between the Earth and the Sun. We cannot see a New Moon because the side of the Moon that is facing us, is not lit by the sun.

A few days after the New Moon, a **Waxing Crescent** can be seen as a thin silver of light. It increases, or "waxes", in size from one day to the next.

When the Moon's right half is lit by the sun, it is called a **First Quarter**. Sometimes, this phase is called Half Moon. You should be able to see a First Quarter Moon about one week after a New Moon.

During the following week, as the Moon waxes, it becomes more than half lit. This phase is called **Waxing Gibbous**.

When the Moon has completed exactly half of its trip around the Earth from the previous new moon, a **Full Moon** occurs. A Full Moon is when we can see the entire lit portion of the Moon because the side of the Moon facing Earth is completely turned towards the Sun.

New Moon

Waxing Crescent

First Quarter

Waxing Gibbous

Full Moon

Phases of the Moon

During a week after Full Moon, the Moon starts to "wane", or decrease in size. The Moon is now in the **Waning Gibbous** phase. The darkness starts to creep in from the right as the left side remains lit.

A **Last Quarter** Moon occurs next when the entire left half side of the Moon is lit.

Finally, during the last week of its monthly orbit, a **Waning Crescent** arrives as the Moon's left side becomes a thin silver of light.

The Moon will be a New Moon again a day or two after a Waning Crescent, and the cycle starts all over again!

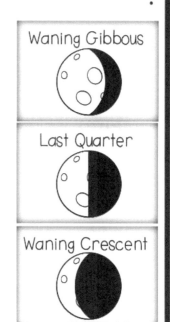

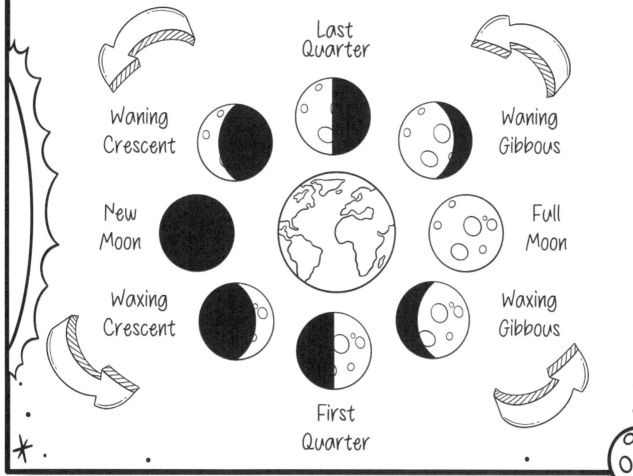

Name: _____

PHASES OF THE MOON

After learning about the phases of the Moon, answer the following questions.

1   Why does the Moon's shape appear to be changing?

    a)   Because it is changing shape
    b)   Due to its rotation around the Earth
    c)   Because of the Earth's shadow
    d)   Due to the moon's brightness

2   How long does it take the Moon to go through the eight different phases?

    a)   7 days
    b)   14 days
    c)   29.5 days
    d)   365 days

3.   Which phase comes after a waxing crescent?

    a)   New Moon
    b)   First Quarter
    c)   Waxing Gibbous
    d)   Full Moon

4.   Which picture shows a Waning Gibbous Moon?

a)   b)

c)   d)

5.   True or False: A waxing Moon appears to be getting smaller. (If false, rewrite the sentence to make it true.)

6.   What is the Moon phase when the Moon has completed exactly half of its trip around the Earth from the previous New Moon?

7.   Why can't we see a New Moon?

Name: _____

MOON PHASES DIAGRAM

Label the phases of the Moon.

Waning Gibbous	New Moon	Full Moon	Last Quarter
Waxing Crescent	Waxing Gibbous	Waning Crescent	First Quarter

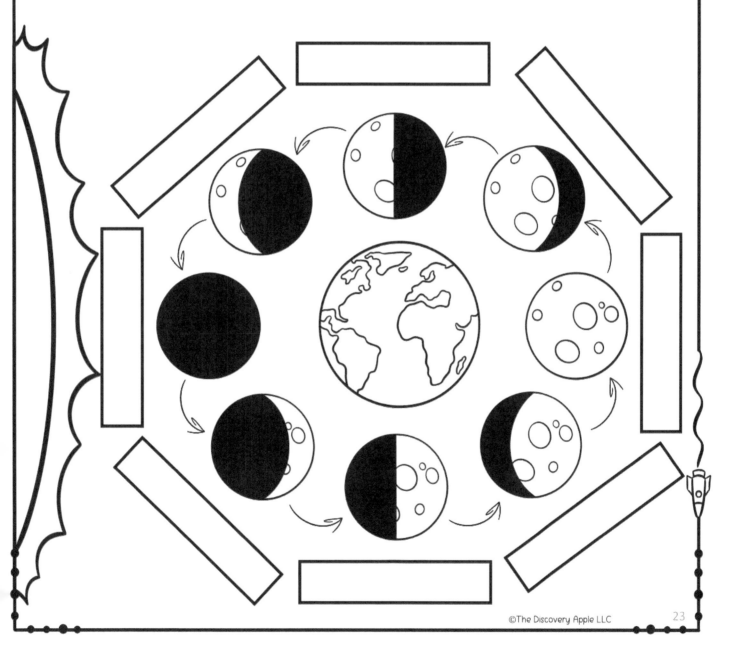

Name: _____

Week Two

LET'S SHADE!

Shade in the circle to show the Moon phase that is written.

1.
Full Moon

2.
New Moon

3.
First quarter

4.
Waxing
Gibbous

5.
Waning
Crescent

6.
Last Quarter

7.
Waxing
Crescent

8.
Waning
Gibbous

9. Is the Moon waxing or waning?

a) Waxing

b) Waning

10. Is the Moon waxing or waning?

a) Waxing

b) Waning

Name: _____

VOCAB MATCH

Match each word to its definition. Write the correct letter in the space provided.

1. Moon _____

2. Phase _____

3. Crescent _____

4. Gibbous _____

5. Quarter _____

6. New Moon _____

7. Full Moon _____

8. Waxing _____

9. Waning _____

A More than half of the Moon is lit
_____

B The list part of the Moon is getting bigger
_____

C One of the different shapes of the Moon is seen from Earth
_____

D The Moon is not visible from Earth
_____

E The entire Moon is lit
_____

F Half of the Moon is lit
_____

G The lit part of the Moon is getting smaller
_____

H Earth's natural satellite
_____

I Less than half of the Moon is lit

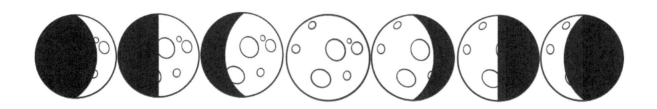

1. If you observe a full moon tonight, what phase will the moon be in about a week? Why?

2. How would moon phases appear different if you were standing on the Moon looking at Earth?

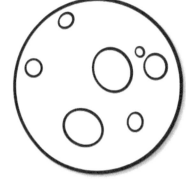

BECOME a MOON SPY!

As you watch the Moon night after night, you'll see
its phases shift, with each phase revealing a new
part of the Moon's surface!

BE A MOON SPY!

Spy on the Moon every night for 30 days. Record the date, shade in the phase you see, and write the phase name.

Date:

Phase:

Date:

Phase:

Date:

Phase:

Date:

Phase:

Date:

Phase:

Date:

Phase:

Date:

Phase:

Date:

Phase:

Date:

Phase:

Date:

Phase:

Date:

Phase:

Date:

Phase:

Date:

Phase:

Date:

Phase:

Date:

Phase:

Date: Phase:	Date: Phase:	Date: Phase:
Date: Phase:	Date: Phase:	Date: Phase:
Date: Phase:	Date: Phase:	Date: Phase:
Date: Phase:	Date: Phase:	Date: Phase:
Date: Phase:	Date: Phase:	Date: Phase:

Let's Reflect!

Based on your observations, can you predict what the moon will look like on a specific date in the future? Explain.

_____

_____

Week Three

Solar AND Lunar ECLIPSES

During a solar eclipse, the Moon perfectly lines up between the Earth and the Sun, creating a spectacular moment when day briefly turns to night!

Week Three

SOLAR AND LUNAR ECLIPSES

Read the passage to complete the tasks for the next few days.

Have you ever wondered what happens when the Sun, the Moon, and the Earth line up perfectly? That's when we get something really cool called an eclipse! There are two main types of eclipses: solar eclipse and lunar eclipse. Let's explore both of them.

Solar Eclipse

A solar eclipse happens when the Moon passes between the Earth and the Sun. This blocks the Sun's light and casts a shadow on the Earth. The eclipse is not visible from everywhere in the world; it can only be seen from places where the shadow falls. In these areas, it appears as though the Sun has gone dark.

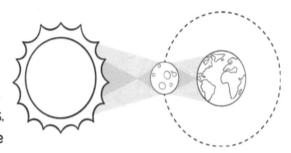

There are three types of solar eclipses:

TOTAL SOLAR ECLIPSE	PARTIAL SOLAR ECLIPSE	ANNULAR SOLAR ECLIPSE
The Moon completely covers the Sun, and it gets dark, like night, for a few minutes. You would see a bright ring around the dark sun, called the corona.	Only part of the Sun is covered by the Moon, so it looks like a chunk is taken out of the Sun	The Moon covers the center of the Sun, leaving a ring of light around the edges. This is sometimes called the "ring of fire."
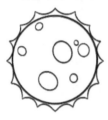		

Always remember to never look directly at a solar eclipse without special glasses. It can damage your eyes! The Sun's rays are so powerful that they can burn your retinas, the sensitive parts at the back of your eyes, which can lead to permanent vision loss. Special eclipse glasses are designed to protect your eyes by blocking out most of the Sun's harmful rays.

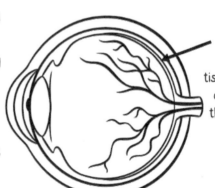

RETINA
The layer of tissue at the back of the eyeball that is sensitive to light

Week Three

Lunar Eclipse

A lunar eclipse happens when the Earth moves between the Sun and the Moon. The Earth blocks the Sun's light, and the shadow falls on the Moon. A lunar eclipse can only occur during a Full Moon.

A lunar eclipse can be viewed over a much larger area on Earth compared to solar eclipses. Since half of the Earth is always in nighttime, a lunar eclipse can be observed by everyone on that side of the planet, covering a wide geographical area.

Unlike solar eclipses, you can view a lunar eclipse without needing special glasses to protect the eyes. During a total lunar eclipse, the Moon often appears reddish in color. This phenomenon is sometimes referred to as a "Blood Moon." This is because the Moon reflects some sunlight that is refracted by the Earth's atmosphere. The light that is refracted is reddish in color, which is why the Moon often appears a dark brownish-red.

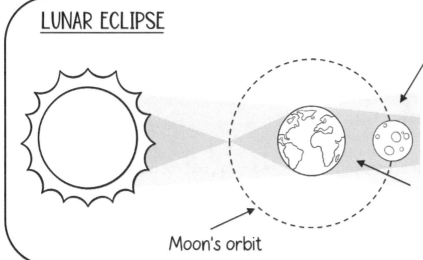

LUNAR ECLIPSE

Penumbra
The outer part of the Earth's shadow where only a portion of the Sun's light is blocked by the Earth

Umbra
The darkest part of Earth's shadow where the Earth completely blocks direct sunlight from reaching the Moon.

Moon's orbit

Eclipses don't happen every month because the orbits of the Earth and the Moon are slightly tilted. The Sun, Earth, and Moon have to be perfectly aligned for an eclipse to occur. This alignment happens only a few times a year.

Did you know that ancient people used to be scared of eclipses because they did not understand what was happening? They thought it was a negative sign from the gods or that something magical or dangerous was going to happen.

Name: _____

Week Three

SOLAR AND LUNAR ECLIPSES

After learning about the solar and lunar eclipses, answer the following questions.

1. Which of the following is true about a total solar eclipse?

   a) The Moon turns reddish in color
   b) The Sun's light is completely blocked by the Moon
   c) It can be observed by everyone on the nighttime side of the Earth
   d) It happens only during a New Moon

2. What happens during a lunar eclipse?

   a) The Moon blocks the Earth's shadow
   b) The Moon passes between the Earth and the Sun
   c) The Sun passes between the Earth and the Moon
   d) The Earth passes between the Sun and the Moon

3. Why do you need special glasses to view a solar eclipse?

   a) The Sun's rays are too powerful and can damage your eyes
   b) The Moon's rays are too powerful and can damage your eyes
   c) The Earth's rays are too powerful and can damage your eyes
   d) The Sun's and the Moon's rays together are too powerful and can damage your eyes.

4. What is a "Blood Moon"?

   a) A total solar eclipse
   b) A type of New Moon
   c) A total lunar eclipse when the Moon appears reddish
   d) A partial lunar eclipse

5. Why is it safe to view a lunar eclipse without special glasses, but not a solar eclipse?

6. Explain why ancient people might have been scared of eclipses and what they thought these events meant.

Name: _____

Week Three

LABEL IT!
Label the diagram.

WORD BANK

Umbra   Earth   Sun

Penumbra   Moon   Moon's Orbit

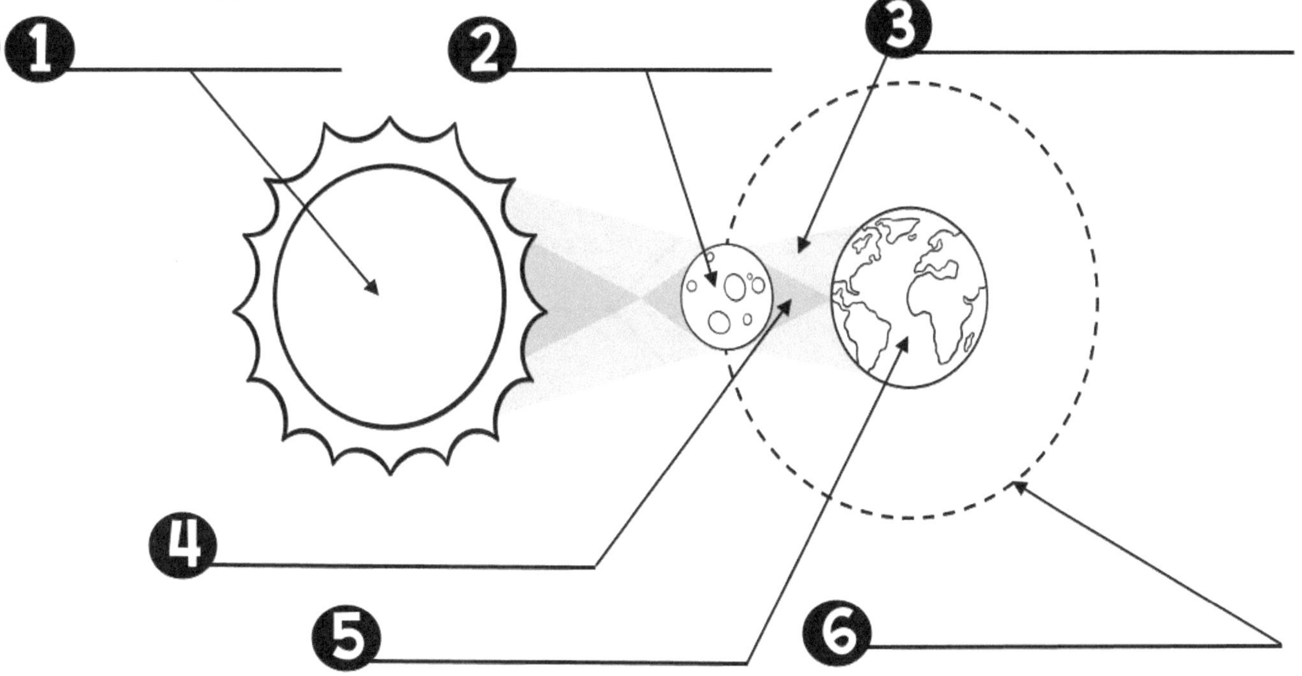

① _____

② _____

③ _____

④

⑤

⑥

SUMMARIZE IT!
Write a summary of what is happening in the diagram shown above.

⑦

Name: _____

Week Three

SOLAR OR LUNAR?

Read each statement carefully and decide if it describes a lunar eclipse or a solar eclipse. Write "Lunar" or "Solar" next to each statement

1 The Sun appears to be partially or completely blocked out for a short period of time. _____

2 The Earth passes between the Sun and the Moon. _____

3. The shadow covers only specific areas on Earth, not the entire planet. _____

4. The Moon passes between the Sun and the Earth _____

5. The Moon can appear to change color, often looking red or orange. _____

6. You can only see this type of eclipse during the night. _____

7. You can view this type of eclipse without needing special glasses. _____

8. You can only see this type of eclipse during the day. _____

9. Can only occur during a full moon. _____

10. You should not look at this eclipse without special glasses. _____

Name: _____

Vocab Match

Match each word with its definition. Write the correct letter in the space provided.

1. Eclipse _____

2. Shadow _____

3. Solar Eclipse _____

4. Lunar Eclipse _____

5. Umbra _____

6. Penumbra _____

7. Total Eclipse _____

8. Partial Eclipse _____

9. Orbit _____

10. Phase _____

A The dark, central part of a shadow where the light is completely blocked.
_____

B The dark shape created when an object blocks light.
_____

C When the light from the Sun or Moon is completely covered by the shadow.
_____

D the path that one object in space follows as it moves around another object.
_____

E When the Moon moves between the Earth and the Sun, blocking out the Sun's light
_____

F When only part of the Sun or Moon is covered by the shadow.
_____

G when one object in space moves into the shadow of another object, making it hard or impossible to see the first object.
_____

H The lighter, outer part of a shadow where only part of the light is blocked.
_____

I A stage in the cycle of the Moon or Sun as seen from Earth.
_____

J When the Earth moves between the Sun and the Moon, casting a shadow on the Moon.

Week Three

Compare and contrast the visual appearance of a total solar eclipse and a total lunar eclipse. What are the main differences and similarities you observe?

Week Four

Life CYCLE of STARS

When a star like our Sun runs out of fuel, it puffs up into a red giant, expanding so much that it could swallow planets in its path.

A CLOSER LOOK AT STARS

Read the passage to complete the tasks for the next few days.

Did you know that there are trillions of stars in the sky? We can't see most of them without a special telescope because of how far away they are. Even with a telescope, you might not be able to see all of the stars in the universe. The universe is so large! The Sun is the closest star to the Earth.

Stars are giant balls of hot, glowing gas, made of mostly Hydrogen and Helium. Stars get very hot because of the intense pressure and heat at their cores, and this leads to nuclear fusion. Nuclear fusion is where hydrogen combine to form a gas called helium, releasing a massive amount of energy in the process. This energy is responsible for the star's heat and brightness.

The Life Cycle of a Star

A small star goes through a different life cycle than a large star. A star, similar to our Sun, begins as a huge cloud of gas and dust known as a stellar nebula. Gravity causes it to collapse, forming a protostar. A protostar is a baby star in the earliest phase of its formation.

Once the star's core heats up to millions of degrees, nuclear fusion begins, and it enters a long phase known as the main sequence. This phase is where stars spend the majority of their lives. Main Sequence stars constantly burns hydrogen for billions of years!

When the hydrogen in its core runs out, the outer layer of the star expands and it becomes a red giant. In about 5 billion years, our Sun will turn into a red giant! The red giant then sheds the outer layer, forming a colorful shell of gas and dust known as the planetary nebula. The leftover core becomes a white dwarf, slowly cooling down.

Larger stars may go through a process that turns them into red supergiants, which will eventually end in a supernova explosion. Depending on how big the star is, what is left behind could either be a neutron star or a mysterious black hole.

Week Four

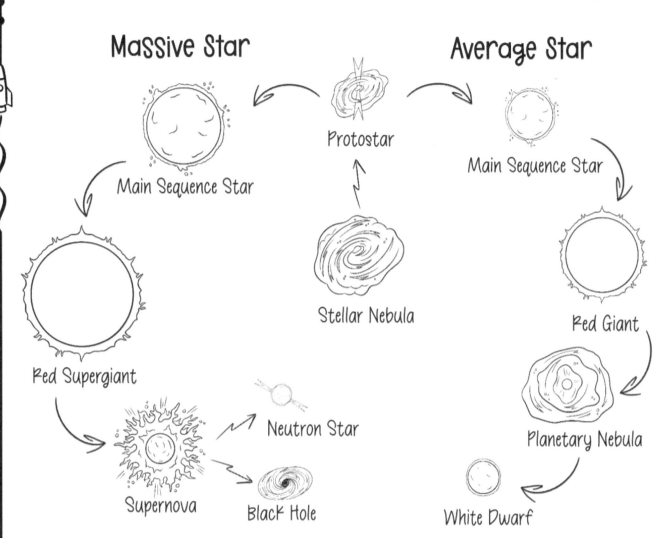

Massive Star

Protostar

Main Sequence Star

Stellar Nebula

Red Supergiant

Supernova

Neutron Star

Black Hole

Average Star

Main Sequence Star

Red Giant

Planetary Nebula

White Dwarf

The Colors of Stars

The stars that are in the Main Sequence phase are categorized by their color. The color of a star reveals its temperature. Blue stars are hotter, while red stars are cooler. If we wanted to see the stars from hottest to coolest, the star colors in order would be: blue, white, yellow, orange, and red.

The bigger the main sequence star, the hotter and brighter they are. The smallest stars are red and are not very bright. Medium-sized stars are yellow with a medium temperature, similar to the Sun. The largest stars are blue and are super bright and hot! The blue stars also burn out the quickest.

Name: _____

A CLOSER LOOK AT STARS

After learning about the stars, answer the following questions.

1. What elements are stars mostly made of?

   a) Oxygen and Carbon
   b) Iron and Nickel
   c) Nitrogen and Argon
   d) Hydrogen and Helium

2. What happens when a star becomes a red giant?

   a) It shrinks and cools down
   b) Its outer layer expands
   c) It turns into a black hole immediately
   d) It stays the same size but gets hotter

3. What happens to a star after it goes through the supernova explosion?

   a) It becomes a red giant
   b) It turns into a white dwarf
   c) It can become either a neutron star or a black hole
   d) It starts the main sequence phase again

4. What color are the hottest stars?

   a) Blue
   b) Yellow
   c) Red
   d) White

5. Describe the difference between a massive star and an average star as they go through their life cycles.

   _____

   _____

   _____

   _____

   _____

   _____

   _____

   _____

Name: _____

Week Four

NUMBER THE LIFE CYCLE OF A MASSIVE STAR

Number the stages in the correct order from 1 to 6, with 1 being the first stage and 6 being the last stage.

PROTOSTAR	RED SUPERGIANT	NEUTRON STAR OR BLACK HOLE

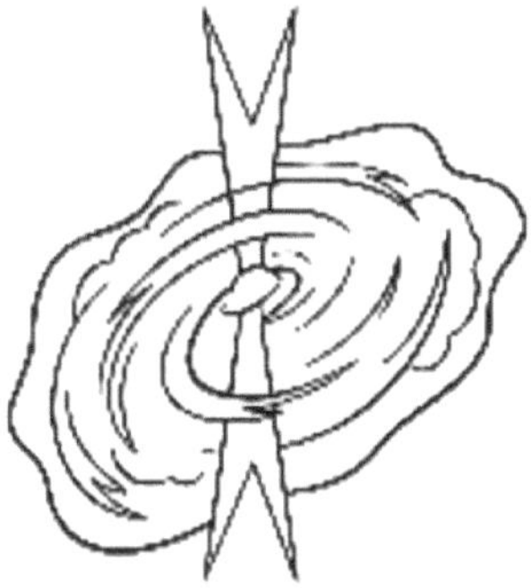

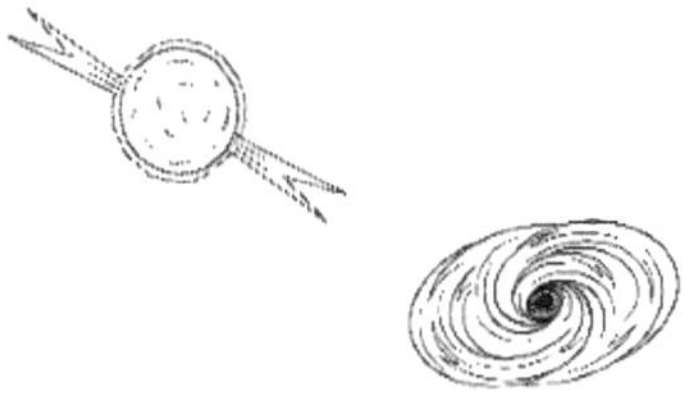

SUPERNOVA	STELLAR NEBULA	MAIN SEQUENCE STAR

Name: _____

CREATE A STAR LIFE CYCLE COMIC STRIP

Think about the different stages in the life cycle of a star. Title each stage and write captions to describe what is happening in each panel. Explain the scientific processes in a fun way. Two of them are already done for you. Add some detail to the illustrations, such as faces or space elements, to make your comic strip more engaging, then color or decorate your comic strip.

1. I'm a Stellar Nebula, and I'm where stars are born!

2.

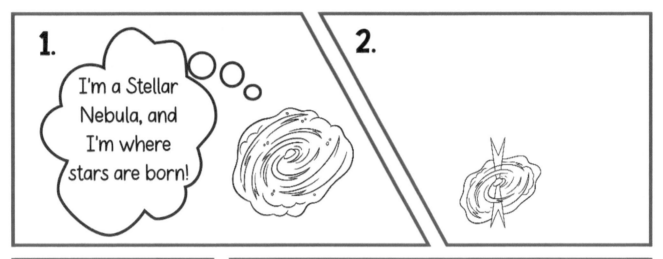

3. I'm a main sequence star, just like the Sun! Ill stay like this for billions of years!

4.

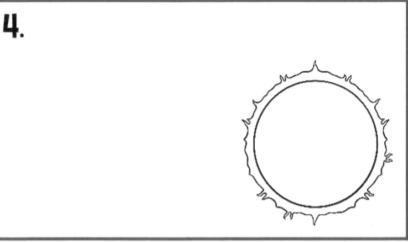

5.

6.

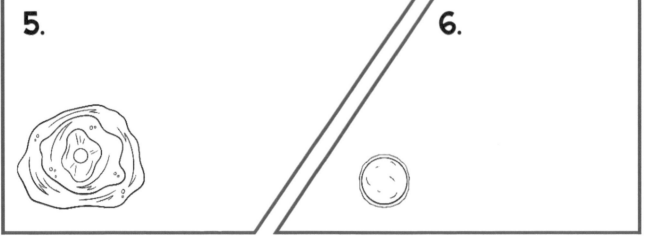

Week Four

Name: _____

VOCAB MATCH

Match each word with its definition. Write the correct letter in the space provided.

1. Nuclear Fusion _____

2. Stellar Nebula _____

3. Protostar _____

4. Main Sequence _____

5. Red Giant _____

6. Planetary Nebula _____

7. White Dwarf _____

8. Black Dwarf _____

9. Black Hole _____

10. Red Supergiant _____

11. Supernova _____

12. Neutron Star _____

A The star has cooled to the point of no longer giving off heat or light

B A baby star that is in the early stage of its formation

C This is what remains after a huge star's core collapses and becomes very dense

D A huge cloud of gas and dust/ this is the first phase of a stars formation

E The largest stars in the universe

F A star, the size of our Sun, that expanded as it runs out of hydrogen

G The long phase in a star's life where nuclear fusion begins

H The leftover core of a star after the planetary nebula phase

I An explosion of a huge star

J Hydrogen combine to form a gas called helium, releasing a massive amount of energy

K A colorful shell of gas and dust that are released by a red giant

L This is what remains after a huge star's core collapses severely and vanishes

Week Four

Write a letter to a friend explaining what happens to a star like our Sun as it grows old and becomes a red giant. Include details about how this change affects the planets around it and why studying the life cycle of stars is important for understanding the universe.

CONSTELLATIONS

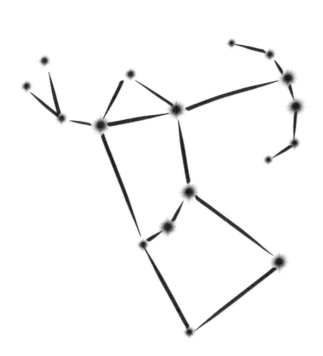

Constellations are like connect-the-dots in the night sky, forming patterns that ancient people imagined as animals, heroes, and mythical creatures!

CONSTELLATIONS
Read the passage to complete the tasks for the next few days.

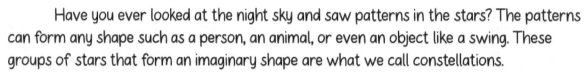

Have you ever looked at the night sky and saw patterns in the stars? The patterns can form any shape such as a person, an animal, or even an object like a swing. These groups of stars that form an imaginary shape are what we call constellations.

The people of ancient Greece were the first to describe constellations. They came up with traditional stories, or myths, for each group of stars that formed an image. For example,. Draco is a constellation known as 'The Dragon' that guarded the golden apples for the Queen of gods. The golden apple tree was a wedding present to Hera when she married Zeus. Draco is one of 88 named constellations.

Draco & Ursa Minor
Constellations

Other than telling stories, early civilization would use the patterns of the stars for practical use. They would use constellations to know where they were and what time of year it was. Farmers depended on the stars to know when it was time to plant and when it was the right time to harvest. Ships were able to travel around the world because of constellations. It allowed for the discovery of America and the spread of European culture.

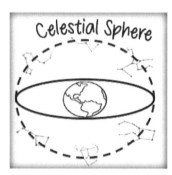

Celestial Sphere

Constellations are always moving naturally as earth moves, so astronomers map out the constellations to help know where everything is at certain times of the year. An imaginary sphere, known as the celestial sphere, is used by astronomers to explain the positions and movements of stars and other objects.

In ancient times, people believed that the stars were attached to the celestial sphere and that they revolved around the Earth in a single day. However, we now know that this is not the case. The apparent motion of the stars from East to West in their tracks is a result of Earth rotating on its axis. While stars do have their own movements, their great distance, makes these motions unnoticeable to the naked eye.

Week Five

Name: _____

CONSTELLATIONS

After learning about the constellations, answer the following questions.

1. **What are constellations?**

    a) Stars that are closer to the Earth
    b) Groups of stars forming an imaginary shape
    c) Planets in our solar system
    d) Satellites orbiting Earth

2. **What does the word "myth" mean?**

    a) Traditional story
    b) Scientific explanation
    c) Recent discovery
    d) Fictional novel

3. **Why did early civilizations use constellations?**

    a) To tell stories
    b) To predict weather changes
    c) To communicate with other civilizations
    d) To know where they were and what time of year it was

4. **What is the celestial sphere?**

    a) A real sphere in space
    b) A planet in our solar system
    c) An imaginary sphere used by astronomers
    d) A new type of star

5. **What is the myth associated with the constellation Draco?**

    a) A giant bear
    b) A dragon that guarded the golden apples
    c) A lion that ruled the sky
    d) A star that lived in the ocean

6. **True or False:** In ancient times, people believed that stars were attached to the celestial sphere and revolved around the Earth.

7. **What causes the apparent motion of stars from East to West in the night sky?**

    a) The Earth is rotating on its axis
    b) The stars are actually moving in that direction
    c) The Sun's light pushes the stars
    d) The wind blows them across the sky

8. **Why are the movements of stars unnoticeable to the naked eye?**

    a) Because stars do not move at all
    b) Because of the Earth's gravity holding them in place
    c) Due to their great distance from Earth
    d) Because they are hidden behind clouds

Name: _____

CREATE A CONSTELLATION!

Connect 6 or more stars to form a constellation of anything you want: It could be an animal, a person, or an object.

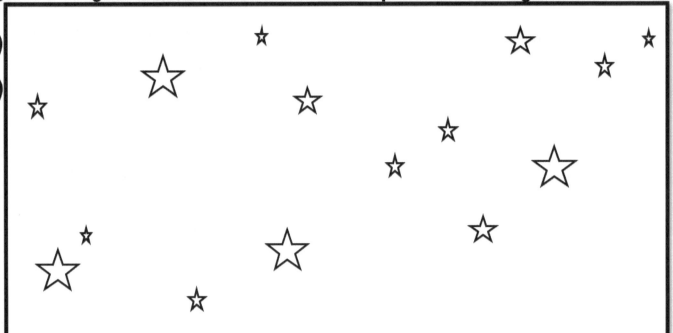

What do you want to name your constellation?

Name:
_____

Also Known As: _____

Write a short story about the constellation you designed.

_____

_____

_____

_____

_____

_____

Name: _____

Week Five

CONSTELLATION MYTHS

Orion

Orion was a skilled hunter, famous for his strength and beauty. According to Greek Mythology, he bragged that he could kill any creature on Earth. This angered the Earth goddess Gaia, who sent a giant scorpion to sting him. After his death, the gods placed him in the sky as a constellation.

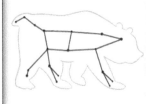

Ursa Major

Ursa Major, also known as "The Great Bear" or "The Big Dipper". According to myth, Callisto, a friend of the goddess Artemis, was transformed into a bear by the jealous Hera. To protect her, Zeus placed her in the sky, where she became Ursa Major.

Draco

Draco, the dragon, guarded the golden apples in the garden of Hesperides. These apples were a wedding gift to Hera, the queen of the gods. Draco was eventually slain by Hercules as one of his 12 labors, and he was placed in the sky as a constellation.

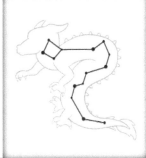

Cygnus

Cygnus is also known as 'The Swan'. One of the most famous myth associated with Cygnus involves the character Leda, Queen of Sparta. Zeus liked Leda. One day, Leda was attacked by an eagle, so he disguised himself as a swan and rescued her.

Cassiopeia

Cassiopeia is also known as 'The Vain Queen'. She bragged that she and her daughter Andromeda were more beautiful than the sea nymphs. This angered the god of the sea, Poseidon, who sent a monster to destroy her kingdom. To save her people, Cassiopeia had to sacrifice her daughter Andromeda. However, Perseus rescued Andromeda by defeating the sea monster. The gods later placed Cassiopeia in the sky as punishment.

Name: _____

Week Five

CONSTELLATION MYTHS

Andromeda

Andromeda was the daughter of Cassiopeia and was saved from a sea monster by the hero Perseus. After Perseus killed the monster, he and Andromeda married, and she was placed in the sky as a constellation.

Pegasus

Pegasus is the winged horse that was born from the blood of Medusa after she was killed by Perseus. Pegasus flew to Mount Olympus and carried thunderbolts for Zeus. He also helped Bellerophon in his adventures, but was stung by a gadfly sent by Zeus when Bellerophon tried to fly to Olympus.

Perseus

Perseus is one of the greatest Greek heroes, known for killing Medusa, the Gorgon whose gaze could turn people to stone. After defeating Medusa, he used her head as a weapon to save Andromeda from a sea monster.

Hercules

Hercules, also known as the strongman, is a famous hero known for completing the twelve nearly impossible labors. The goddess Hera caused Hercules to lose his mind and do terrible things. As punishment, the King Eurystheus, ordered Hercules to complete the 12 extremely difficult and dangerous tasks. He successfully completed them all, showing his incredible strength and bravery. .

Canis Major

Canis Major, meaning "Greater Dog", represents the dog Laelaps, who was a gift to Orion. Laelaps was known for his incredible speed and loyalty. According to myth, Zeus placed him in the sky as a constellation to run eternally after the hare (represented by the constellation Lepus).

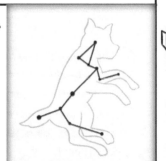

WHO AM I? (CONSTELLATIONS)

① I was going on adventures with Bellerophon until I got stung by a gadfly.

② I am also known as 'The Big Dipper'.

③ I was saved by Perseus from a sea monster.

④ I was a gift to Orion and I am known for my speed and loyalty.

⑤ I guarded the golden apples of Hesperides.

⑥ I was known for the twelve labors.

⑦ I bragged that my daughter was more beautiful than the sea nymphs.

⑧ I was known for killing Medusa.

⑨ I am a skilled hunter and I got stung by a scorpion.

⑩ I was placed among the stars as a swan.

Draco

Andromeda

Perseus

Orion

Cygnus

Canis Major

Ursa Major

Hercules

Pegasus

Cassiopeia

Name: _____

Week Five

VOCAB MATCH

Match each word with its definition. Write the correct letter in the space provided.

1. Constellation _____

2. Astrologer _____

3. Cluster _____

4. Star _____

5. Myth _____

6. Celestial Sphere _____

A A group of similar stars close together

_____

B An imaginary sphere that is used by astronomers to explain the positions and movements of stars and other objects

C A person who studies the positions of the stars and planets in the sky and believes that it can have an impact on their personality and behavior

D A massive ball of gas that emits light and heat, often forming part of a constellation

E A group of stars that form a pattern in the sky

_____

F A traditional story that a group of people believed to be real

Also Known As...

WORD BANK   The Winged Horse   The Captive Princess   The Swan

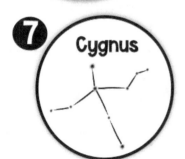
7 Cygnus

8 Andromeda

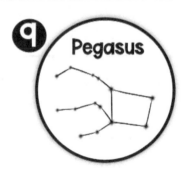
9 Pegasus

_____   _____   _____

Week Five

Different cultures around the world have different names and stories for the same constellations. Why do you think that? What does that tell us about how people view the night sky?

Week Six

Comets, METEORS,  and ASTEROIDS

Comets, meteors, and asteroids all have this thing in common—they're fascinating space rocks that give us a glimpse of the wonders of our solar system!

Week Six

COMETS, METEORS, AND ASTEROIDS

Read the passage to complete the tasks for the next few days.

Did you know that there are all kinds of "space rocks" zooming around our solar system? Three of the most interesting ones are comets, meteors, and asteroids!

COMETS

Comets are often called 'dirty snowballs' because the solid center of a comet, called the nucleus, is made up of ice, dust, and rocks. As a comet gets closer to the Sun, the heat causes the ice in the nucleus to turn into gas, forming a bright, glowing 'head' around the comet called a 'coma.' As the comet zooms through space, the gases will trail behind the comet, forming two tails: a **gas tail** and a **dust tail**, which can stretch out for millions of miles. The gas tail always points directly away from the sun due to the solar wind, while the dust tail curves slightly along the comet's orbit. You can sometimes see comets in the night sky as they pass Earth, and they look like a bright ball with a long, glowing tail.

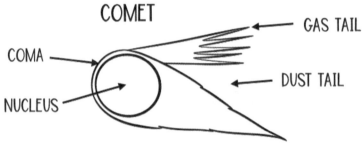

METEORS

Meteors are often called "shooting stars," but they're not really stars at all! Before entering Earth's atmosphere, they are known as meteoroids—tiny pieces of dust or rock floating in space. When a meteoroid enters the atmosphere, it travels so fast that it creates a streak of light as it burns up, and that's what we see as a meteor. When many meteors appear at the same time and in the same area of the sky, it's called a meteor shower. Most meteors are very small and burn up completely before they reach the ground. But if a meteor makes it all the way to Earth's surface, we call it a meteorite.

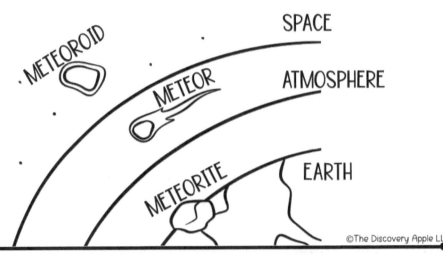

Week Six

ASTEROIDS

Asteroids are big chunks of rock that orbit the Sun, just like planets do. Most asteroids are found in the asteroid belt, which is a region between Mars and Jupiter. There are millions of asteroids of different sizes within this belt. Some are small, like a pebble, while others can be hundreds of miles wide.

There is still so much to discover about asteroids, comets, and meteorites. Scientists around the world continue to study these fascinating space rocks to learn more about the history of our solar system. Every year, new asteroids and comets are discovered, each one given a unique name and added to our growing understanding of the universe. These discoveries remind us that space is full of mysteries, and there is always more to explore and learn. Who knows? Maybe one day, you'll be the one to make the next big discovery in space!

Week Six

Name: _____

COMETS, METEORS, AND ASTEROIDS

After learning about the comets, meteors, and asteroids, answer the following questions.

1. What is a comet mostly made of?

    a) Metal and rock
    b) Ice, dust, and rocks
    c) Water and soil
    d) Only gases

2. What happens to a meteoroid when it enters Earth's atmosphere?

    a) It burns up and creates a streak of light
    b) It turns into an asteroid
    c) It grows larger
    d) It freezes

3. Where are most asteroids found in our solar system?

    a) Between Earth and Mars
    b) Near the Sun
    c) Outside the solar system
    d) Between Mars and Jupiter

4. What is a meteorite?

    a) A meteor that burns up in the atmosphere
    b) A small asteroid orbiting the Sun
    c) A meteoroid that reaches Earth's surface
    d) A comet without a tail

5. Meteor showers happen when many meteors appear in the sky at the same time. Have you ever seen a meteor shower? If so, describe what it was like. If not, would you like to see one? Why do you think people find meteor showers so fascinating?

_____

_____

_____

_____

_____

_____

_____

Name: _____

Week Six

COMET, METEOR, OR ASTEROID?

Identify whether each statement is describing comet, meteor, or asteroid
and put a check mark under the correct category.

		COMET	METEOR	ASTEROID
1.	known for having a bright, glowing tail that can be seen from Earth			
2.	a small, rocky body that orbits the sun, often found in a belt between Mars and Jupiter			
3.	often called a "shooting star" when it burns up in Earth's atmosphere			
4.	If this object reaches Earth's surface without burning up, it is called a meteorite.			
5.	this can be as small as a pebble and can also be hundreds of miles wide			
6.	mostly made of ice, dust, and rocks			
7.	can be seen as a streak of light in the night sky when it burns up in the atmosphere			
8.	Develops a coma as it nears the Sun			

Name: _____

Week Six

FILL IN THE BLANKS

Fill in the blanks with the correct answers and find the words
(your answers) in the word search on the next page.

1. _____ are often called "dirty snowball" because they are made of ice, dust, and rocks.

2. When a comet gets close to the Sun, it develops a glowing head called a

_____.

3. The tail of a comet always points _____ from the Sun due to the

solar wind.

4. If a meteor survives its journey through the atmosphere and reaches Earth's surface, it is called a

_____.

5. The _____ Belt, located between Mars and Jupiter, contains

millions of rocky objects.

6. Asteroids _____ the Sun just like planets.

7. Comets have two tails: a gas tail and a _____ tail, both of

which become visible as they approach the Sun.

8. Most _____ are small and burn up completely before they

reach the Earth's surface.

9. A meteor _____ occurs when many meteors appear in the sky at

the same time and from the same direction.

10. Scientists around the world continue to study space rocks to learn more about the

_____ of our solar system.

Name: _____

Week Six

FIND YOUR ANSWERS

Find the answers you wrote on the previous page in the word search.

C	E	C	A	D	U	E	N	E	C	O	M	A	T
A	S	E	P	S	O	P	E	I	T	I	M	S	G
M	H	A	B	D	T	U	M	A	S	I	I	N	B
O	O	W	D	C	M	E	T	E	O	R	S	L	E
U	W	L	M	A	C	S	R	O	N	E	R	G	H
F	E	A	S	R	P	O	Y	O	I	C	A	L	A
L	R	O	Y	S	R	T	M	R	I	I	T	N	V
A	I	S	P	Y	E	O	E	E	T	D	I	S	I
H	O	R	A	M	D	L	T	T	T	O	O	F	O
E	I	W	E	E	A	B	E	E	I	S	N	S	R
Y	A	S	E	R	T	I	O	O	R	O	F	I	T
D	S	B	T	Y	O	V	R	U	Z	Z	N	I	L
U	H	I	B	O	R	N	I	T	I	O	B	Q	N
S	R	A	V	F	R	Y	T	U	V	R	G	Z	L
T	H	O	J	E	R	Y	E	N	O	A	D	F	R
E	H	K	L	I	U	O	F	X	L	O	B	Y	I

Name: _____

Vocab Match

Match each word with its definition. Write the correct letter in the space provided.

1. Asteroid _____
2. Comet _____
3. Meteor _____
4. Meteorite _____
5. Meteoroid _____
6. Coma _____
7. Nucleus _____
8. Asteroid Belt _____
9. Solar Wind _____
10. Orbit _____

A A streak of light in the sky, often called a "shooting star," caused by a meteoroid burning up in Earth's atmosphere.

B The glowing head of a comet, formed when its ice turns into gas as it gets closer to the Sun.

C A "dirty snowball" made of ice, dust, and rocks that orbits the Sun and develops a glowing tail when near the Sun.

D The path an object takes as it moves around a star, planet, or moon.

E A large rock in space that orbits the Sun, mostly found in the asteroid belt.

F A region in space between Mars and Jupiter where most asteroids are found.

G A piece of a meteoroid that survives its trip through Earth's atmosphere and lands on the ground.

H The solid center of a comet, made of ice and rock.

I A stream of charged particles released from the Sun that can push the tail of a comet.

J A small rock or particle in space, smaller than an asteroid.

Week Six

Write a letter to a friend explaining the difference between an asteroid, a meteor, and a comet. Use examples to help explain how each one behaves differently in space.

Week Seven

GRAVITY

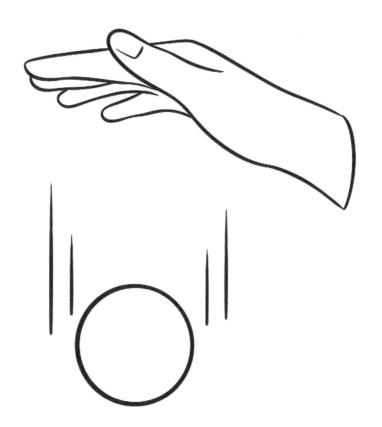

Gravity is like an invisible glue that keeps us and everything else stuck to the Earth, preventing us from floating away into space!

Week Seven

UNDERSTANDING GRAVITY IN SPACE
Read the passage to complete the tasks for the next few days.

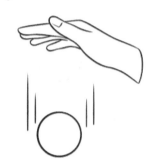

Have you ever wondered why, when you jump, you don't keep floating off into space? The answer lies in understanding gravity. Gravity is a force that pulls objects toward each other. It's also what keeps you on Earth instead of drifting away into space! On Earth, gravity pulls everything down toward the center of the planet, which is why objects fall when you let go of them.

In space, gravity plays a huge role in how everything moves. The sun, being the largest object in the solar system, has the most gravity. Its gravity is so strong that it pulls all the planets, including Earth, into orbits around it, keeping them from flying off into space.

The moon also has gravity, which is why it stays in orbit around Earth. The moon's gravity even affects the tides in our oceans. When the moon is closer to one side of Earth, it pulls on the water, causing high tides.

Every object in space has some gravity, even if it's just a little. Larger objects, like planets and stars, have stronger gravitational forces because they have more mass compared to smaller objects, such as moons, asteroids, or space debris. Mass is the amount of matter an object has. The more mass an object has, the stronger its gravitational pull. Because of this, smaller objects are pulled toward things with much greater mass.

Gravity pulls all objects toward the Earth at the same rate, regardless of their mass. This means that if you drop a feather and a rock at the same time in a vacuum chamber (where there's no air), they would hit the ground at the same time! However, air resistance on Earth makes lighter objects like feathers fall more slowly.

Gravity also gets weaker the farther you are from an object. That's why you would weigh less on the Moon than you do on Earth—the Moon has less mass, and therefore, less gravity.

Without gravity, there wouldn't be orbits, and the planets, moons, and even galaxies wouldn't stay in place. It's one of the most important forces in the universe, making sure everything moves in the right way and stays where it's supposed to be.

Name: _____

Week Seven

Day 1

UNDERSTANDING GRAVITY IN SPACE

After learning about the gravity, answer the following questions.

1. **What is gravity?**

    a) A force that pushes objects away from each other
    b) A force that pulls objects toward each other
    c) A force that only affects large objects
    d) A force that only exists in space

2. **Why do objects fall to the ground when you let go of them on Earth?**

    a) Because of the wind
    b) Because of air resistance
    c) Because of gravity
    d) Because they have mass

3. **Why does the moon stay in orbit around the Earth?**

    a) Because of Earth's gravity
    b) Because it has not gravity
    c) Because of its speed
    d) Because its close to the sun

4. **What happens to objects when they move farther away from a big object with strong gravity?**

    a) They weigh more
    b) They have the same weight
    c) They disappear
    d) They weigh less

5. Explain why gravity is important in the solar system. How does it affect the movement of planets?

GRAVITATIONAL PULL

Number the objects from 1 to 5, where '1' represents the object with the greatest gravitational pull and '5' represents the object with the least gravitational pull.

THE MOON

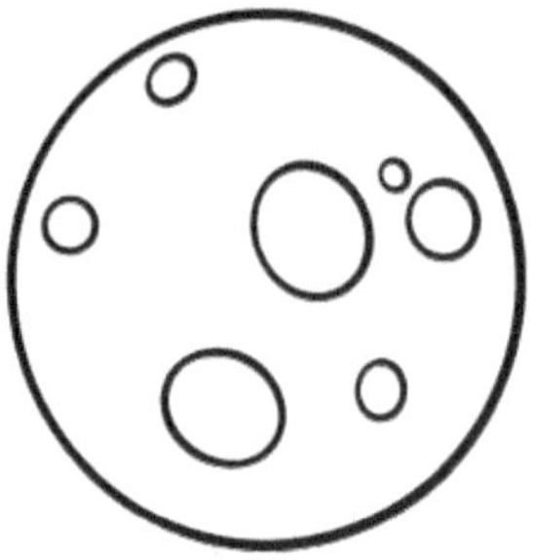

A CAR

THE SUN

AN ASTEROID

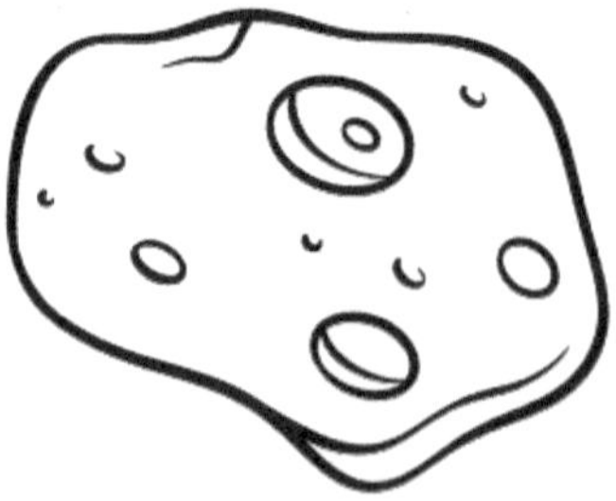

A BASEBALL

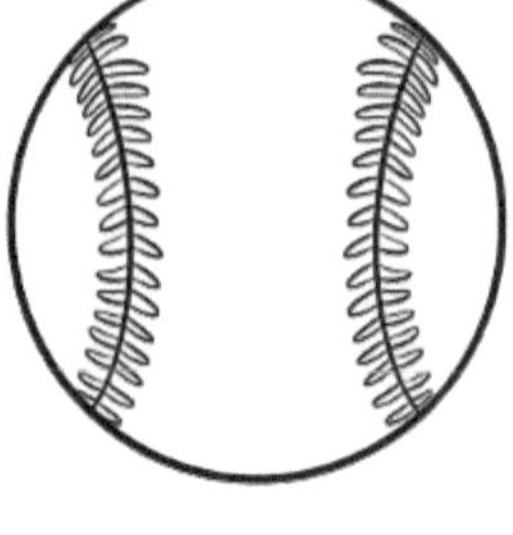

EARTH

Name: _____

Week Seven

TRUE OR FALSE

Mark each statement as true or false.
Extension: For the false statements, rewrite each sentence on a sheet of paper to make it true.

	True	False
1. Gravity is a force that pushes objects away from each other.	☐	☐
2. Gravity is what keeps the planets in orbit around the Sun.	☐	☐
3. Gravity affects the tides in Earth's oceans by pulling on the water.	☐	☐
4. Gravity only affects objects that are in motion.	☐	☐
5. The Moon's gravity is weaker than Earth's gravity.	☐	☐
6. An object's weight and mass are the same on every planet.	☐	☐
7. Gravity only exists on planets and not in space.	☐	☐
8. Earth's gravity is what causes objects to fall toward the ground when dropped.	☐	☐
9. Without gravity, objects in space would eventually stop moving.	☐	☐
10. The gravitational force between two objects decreases as the distance between them increases.	☐	☐

Name: _____

Week Seven

Vocab Match

Match each word with its definition. Write the correct letter in the space provided.

1. Gravity _____

2. Mass _____

3. Weight _____

4. Acceleration _____

5. Air Resistance _____

6. Tides _____

7. Force _____

8. Orbit _____

9. Microgravity _____

10. Free Fall _____

(A) The rate at which an object's velocity changes due to forces like gravity.

(B) The amount of matter in an object, which affects how much gravity it experiences.

(C) The force of air pushing against a moving object, which can affect how gravity influences its motion.

(D) The curved path an object takes as it moves around another object due to gravity.

(E) The rise and fall of sea levels caused by the gravitational pull of the Moon and the Sun on Earth's oceans.

(F) The force that pulls objects toward the center of the Earth or any other object with mass.

(G) The motion of an object when it is falling solely under the influence of gravity, with no other forces acting on it.

(H) The measure of the force of gravity on an object.

(I) A condition in which objects appear to be weightless and experience very weak gravitational forces, often found in space.

(J) A push or pull that can cause an object to move, stop, or change direction.

Week Seven

1. Explain what you think would happen if Earth's gravity suddenly became weaker? How might that also affect the way we move?

2. How does gravity help us when we throw a ball into the air? What do you think would happen if there was no gravity?

Week Eight

EARTH'S Rotation

AND Revolution

While Earth rotates to give us day and night, it also travels around the Sun in a year-long journey, completing one full revolution every 365 days!

Week Eight

SPINNING THROUGH SPACE

Read the passage to complete the tasks for the next few days.

Did you know that the Earth is always moving? You don't feel like it is constantly moving, but it is! It spins and it moves around the Sun. The spinning of the Earth is called **rotation**. The Earth has an imaginary line, or **axis**, that starts at the north pole and goes through Earth's center ending at the south pole. The Earth spins on this axis. It takes the Earth about 24 hours, or one day, to make one complete rotation on its axis.

While the Earth rotates, different parts of the planet faces the Sun. As one side faces the Sun, the other side faces away from the Sun. When the United States has daytime, China has night time because it is on the other side of the planet. The rotation of the Earth also makes the Sun appear to rise in the east and set in the west. The Sun is a star that does not move, but because of the way the Earth turns, the Sun will appear like it is rising in the east and setting in the west.

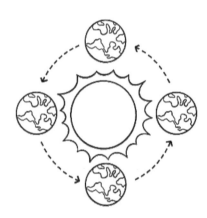

As Earth rotates on its axis, it is also revolving around the Sun. The Earth makes an entire trip around the Sun and never stops. We call this the Earth's **revolution**. The path Earth follows is called its **orbit**. The Earth's orbit is not a perfect circle; instead, it is an elliptical shape, which means it is slightly stretched out like an oval. It takes the Earth 365 ¼ days to revolve around, or orbit, the Sun once. This is the reason we have 365 days in a year.

Throughout the year, as Earth orbits the Sun, many parts of the Earth experience changing **seasons**. Summers are warm and winters are cold. Earth has seasons because of its tilted axis as it travels around the Sun. Its tilt is always pointed in the same direction and never changes. The areas pointing toward the Sun receive more heat than the areas pointing away from the Sun. That area is enjoying summer while the area pointing away from the Sun has winter.

Name: _____

SPINNING THROUGH SPACE

After learning about the earth's rotation and revolution, answer the following questions.

1. How does the tilt of Earth's axis affect the seasons?

   a) It causes the Earth to rotate faster in summer and slower in winter.
   b) It changes the amount of sunlight each hemisphere receives, leading to different seasons.
   c) It makes the Sun move closer to the Earth during summer and farther away in winter.
   d) It has no effect; seasons are caused by the distance between Earth and the Sun.

2. What would happen if Earth's axis were not tilted at all?

   a) The Earth would have the same season all year long
   b) The days would be longer during the winter and shorter during the summer.
   c) The Sun would not rise or set, staying in the same place in the sky.
   d) The Earth would rotate slower, and the year would become shorter.

3. How long does it take the Earth to complete one full rotation?

   a) 365 days
   b) 24 hours
   c) 12 hours
   d) 1 month

4. Why does the Sun appear to rise in the east and set in the west?

   a) Because the Sun moves around the Earth
   b) Because the Earth revolves around the Sun
   c) Because the Earth's axis is tilted
   d) Because the Earth rotates on its axis

5. Imagine you are an astronaut observing Earth from space. How would you explain the difference between Earth's rotation and revolution to someone who has never been to Earth?

_____

_____

_____

_____

_____

_____

Week Eight

Name: _____

TRUE OR FALSE

Read each sentence and mark the appropriate box to indicate whether it is true or false.

		True	**False**
1.	The Earth spins on its axis.	☐	☐
2.	The Earth orbits around the Moon.	☐	☐
3.	It takes the Earth 24 hours to do a complete spin on its axis.	☐	☐
4.	The Earth spins around from west to east.	☐	☐
5.	The path Earth follows is called its rotation.	☐	☐
6.	Revolution is the movement of Earth around the Sun.	☐	☐
7.	It takes the Earth 345 ¼ days to orbit the Sun.	☐	☐
8.	When the northern hemisphere is tilted away from the Sun, it experiences summer.	☐	☐
9.	The top part of the Earth is called the southern hemisphere.	☐	☐
10.	Seasons are caused by Earth's tilted axis as it travels around the Sun.	☐	☐

Week Eight

Name: _____

EARTH'S ROTATION AND REVOLUTION CROSSWORD

Fill in the crossword puzzle using the clues provided. All answers are related to Earth's rotation and revolution.

ACROSS

2. – The time it takes for Earth to complete one full revolution around the Sun.

5. – The path Earth follows as it revolves around the Sun.

6. – The star at the center of our solar system that Earth orbits around.

7. – The spinning of Earth on its axis, causing day and night.

8. – The four periods of the year caused by Earth's revolution and its tilted axis.

10. – The angle of Earth's axis, which affects the seasons.

DOWN

1. – The period of time when one part of Earth is facing the Sun.

3. – Earth's movement around the Sun, taking about 365 days.

4. – The period of time when one part of Earth is turned away from the Sun.

9. – The imaginary line Earth spins around.

Week Eight

Name: _____

VOCAB MATCH

Match each word with its definition. Write the correct letter in the space provided.

1. Rotation _____

2. Revolution _____

3. Axis _____

4. Orbit _____

5. Tilt _____

6. Hemisphere _____

7. Seasons _____

8. Equator _____

9. Elliptical _____

A the path that an object follows as it moves around another object due to gravity

B The oval shape of Earth's orbit around the Sun

C The movement of one abject around another object in a circular or elliptical path

D An imaginary line that divides the Earth into Northern and Southern Hemispheres

E Leaning on one side

F The spinning motion of an object around its own axis

G Half of the Earth, usually divided into Northern and Southern or Eastern and Western

H an imaginary line around which an object rotates or spins

I periods of the year marked by distinct weather patterns and daylight hours, caused by Earth's tilt on its axis and its orbit around the Sun

1. How would life on Earth be different if the planet did not rotate on its axis?

2. If you could design a planet with a unique rotation or orbit, what would it look like, and how would it affect the seasons or day and night?

Week Nine

The HISTORY of Space EXPLORATION

Laika's journey into space was the first time any living creature had been sent to orbit, marking a significant moment in our quest to explore beyond Earth.

Week Nine

THE HISTORY OF SPACE EXPLORATION

Read the passage to complete the tasks for the next few days.

Space exploration is an exciting journey that humans have been on for many years. It all started in the 1950s when scientists and engineers began launching rockets to learn more about space. One of the first big events was in 1957 when the Soviet Union, a group of many countries that used to be united, including Russia, sent a satellite called **Sputnik 1** into space. Sputnik was the first man-made object to circle the planet, and it amazed the world. It showed that we could reach beyond our planet

SPUTNIK 1

LAIKA

A month later, they launched Sputnik 2 carrying a dog named **Laika**. Laika was the first animal launched into space and orbit Earth. Sadly, Laika did not survive her mission. Scientists believe that she died a few hours after launch due to overheating. Sputnik 2, the spacecraft that carried Laika, continued to orbit Earth for about 5 months before it eventually re-entered the atmosphere and burned up. Laika's mission provided valuable information about the effects of space travel on living beings, even though her story had a tragic end.

Soon after, the United States joined the space race by launching **Explorer 1** in 1958. Explorer 1 was the first American satellite and it helped scientists discover the Van Allen radiation belts around Earth. These belts are layers of charged particles that protect us from harmful space radiation. After more than 58,000 orbits, Explorer 1 entered Earth's atmosphere and burned up.

EXPLORER 1

NEIL ARMSTRONG

As space exploration continued, humans were ready to go to space themselves. The United States made history in 1969 when NASA's **Apollo 11** mission successfully landed the first humans on the Moon; **Neil Armstrong** and Buzz Aldrin. Neil Armstrong was the first person to set foot on the Moon, and his famous words, "That's one small step for man, one giant leap for mankind," were heard around the world. This Moon landing was one of the most significant achievements in space exploration.

Week Nine

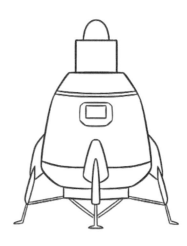

However, not all missions went as planned. In 1970, **Apollo 13** was on its way to the Moon when an oxygen tank exploded, putting the astronauts in serious danger. They were on the third day of their mission and nearly 300,000 miles from Earth. The mission had to be aborted, but thanks to the teamwork of the astronauts and NASA's engineers, all three astronauts returned safely to Earth. The story of Apollo 13 is a powerful example of problem-solving and courage in space.

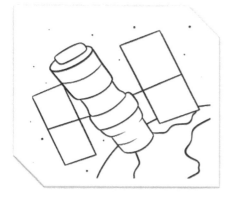

Space exploration didn't stop with the Moon. In 1990, NASA launched the **Hubble Space Telescope**, a powerful telescope that orbits Earth and takes stunning pictures of our universe. Hubble has helped us see distant galaxies that are trillions of miles away, discover new planets, and understand more about the stars and space.

In summary, space exploration has been an incredible journey. As humans have explored the universe with telescopes and launched satellites into space, we've come a long way in understanding the mysteries of space. New missions are being planned all the time, and who knows what amazing discoveries the future will bring!

Week Nine

Name: _____

THE HISTORY OF SPACE EXPLORATION

After learning about the history of space exploration, answer the following questions.

1. **What event marked the beginning of space exploration in the passage?**

   a) The launch of Apollo 11
   b) The launch of Sputnik 1
   c) The discovery of the Van Allen Belts
   d) The launch of the Hubble Space Telescope

2. **Who was Laika?**

   a) The first human to orbit Earth
   b) An American astronaut
   c) A scientist who worked on Sputnik
   d) The first dog to orbit Earth

3. **What was the significance of Explorer 1?**

   a) It discovered the Van Allen radiation belts
   b) It discovered galaxies very far away
   c) It carried the first human to the Moon
   d) It was the first spacecraft to orbit the Moon

4. **Which mission successfully landed the first humans on the Moon?**

   a) Apollo 13
   b) Sputnik 1
   c) Apollo 11
   d) Explorer 1

5. **Who was the first person to set foot on the Moon?**

   a) Yuri Gagarin
   b) Alan Shepard
   c) Neil Armstrong
   d) Sally Ride

6. **What happened during the Apollo 13 mission?**

   a) An oxygen tank exploded, but the astronauts returned safely
   b) The mission successfully landed on the Moon
   c) The mission discovered new planets
   d) It discovered the Van Allen Belts

7. **What is the Hubble Space Telescope used for?**

   a) Launching astronauts into space
   b) Taking pictures of the universe
   c) Landing on other planets
   d) Communicating with satellites

8. **What is the main idea of the passage?**

   a) The history of NASA
   b) The dangers of space exploration
   c) The significant milestones in space exploration history
   d) The discovery of new planets and galaxies

Week Nine

Name: _____

PLAN YOUR OWN SPACE MISSION

Imagine you are the mission commander planning your own space exploration mission. Use your creativity and knowledge to design a successful mission.

MISSION OBJECTIVE

What is the goal of your space mission? Choose one of the following or come up with your own idea and write it down.

- ❏ Landing on Mars
- ❏ Studying a distant moon
- ❏ Exploring an asteroid
- ❏ Searching for life on one of Jupiter's moons
- ❏ Launching a new space telescope

- ❏ Your own idea: _____

_____
_____

DESCRIBE THE MISSION OBJECTIVE:

Example: My mission will explore the surface of Mars to reach for signs of past or present life and collect soil samples.

_____
_____
_____
_____
_____
_____
_____
_____
_____
_____

EQUIPMENT AND SUPPLIES

What equipment or supplies will you bring? Think about what you need to accomplish your mission.

- TOOLS (Examples: Drills, cameras):

_____
_____

- LIFE SUPPORT (Example: oxygen tanks):

_____

- FOOD AND WATER:

_____

- OTHER SUPPLIES:

_____
_____

Week Nine

Name: _____

PLAN YOUR OWN SPACE MISSION

CHALLENGES AND SOLUTIONS

○ What challenges might your mission face? How will you overcome them?

CHALLENGE 1: Running out of Oxygen

SOLUTION: _____
_____

CHALLENGE 1: Equipment Failure

○ SOLUTION: _____
_____

CHALLENGE 3: _____
_____

SOLUTION: _____
_____

○ _____

CREW SELECTION

Who will be on your team? Consider the skills needed for your mission.

ASTRONAUT 1:
_____

ASTRONAUT 2:
_____

ASTRONAUT 3:
_____

Why did you choose these crew members?
_____
_____
_____

MISSION SUCCESS

How will you know if your mission is successful? What are the signs of success? One example of success is that all crew members returned safely to Earth.

_____
_____
_____
_____
_____
_____

NAME YOUR SPACESHIP:

_____

DRAW AND COLOR YOUR SPACESHIP

Week Nine

Day 3

Name: _____

VOCAB MATCH

Match each word with its definition. Write the correct letter in the space provided.

1. Satellite _____

2. Orbit _____

3. Astronaut _____

4. Rocket _____

5. Launch _____

6. Spacecraft _____

7. Telescope _____

8. Mission _____

9. Explore _____

10. Discovery _____

(A) A person who is trained to travel and work in space.
_____

(B) To travel in or through an unfamiliar area to learn more about it.
_____

(C) The path an object takes as it moves around a planet, star, or moon.
_____

(D) A vehicle or device designed for travel or operation in outer space.
_____

(E) An object that orbits around a planet or another celestial body.
_____

(F) An instrument used to observe distant objects by collecting light
_____

(G) A vehicle designed to propel itself by ejecting exhaust gas from one end.
_____

(H) The act of finding or learning something for the first time, often in a scientific context.
_____

(I) A specific task or goal assigned to a spacecraft, such as landing on the Moon or exploring another planet.
_____

(J) The process of sending a spacecraft, satellite, or rocket into space.

Week Nine

Name: _____

SPACE EXPLORATION TIMELINE

Use the key events provided to create a timeline of significant moments in space exploration history. Then, write a brief description or fact about each event.

Key Events

Explorer 1 launched	Sputnik 1 launched	Apollo 13 mission
Hubble Space Telescope launched	Sputnik 2 launched	Apollo 11 Moon landing

OCTOBER 4, 1957

Event: _____

Fact: _____

_____

_____

NOVEMBER 3, 1957

Event: _____

Fact: _____

_____

_____

JANUARY 31, 1958

Event: _____

Fact: _____

_____

_____

JULY 20, 1969

Event: _____

Fact: _____

_____

_____

APRIL 11-17, 1970

Event: _____

Fact: _____

_____

_____

APRIL 24, 1990

Event: _____

Fact: _____

_____

1. Which space exploration event do you think was the most significant? Explain your reasoning using what you've learned.

2. What do you think the future of space exploration might include?

With each new **FACT LEARNED,** You get closer to **UNCOVERING** the mysteries of the **UNIVERSE.**

ANSWER

Keys

Answer Keys

Page 13 – Day 1

1. Uranus
2. Mercury
3. Earth
4. Saturn
5. Jupiter
6. Mars
7. Neptune
8. Venus

Page 14 – Day 2

1. Mercury – terrestrial
2. Venus – terrestrial
3. Earth – terrestrial
4. Mars - terrestrial
5. Jupiter – Gas Giant
6. Saturn - Gas Giant
7. Uranus - Gas Giant
8. Neptune - Gas Giant

Page 15 – Day 3

1. C
2. B
3. B
4. A
5. False: Earth is closer to the Sun than Mars.
6. Terrestrial planets are small, rocky, and have solid surfaces. They include Mercury, Venus, Earth, and Mars. Gas giants, on the other hand, are large and made mostly of gases. They include Jupiter, Saturn, Uranus, and Neptune.
7. Example Response (Answers will vary depending on the planet they choose): Jupiter is unique because it is the largest planet in our solar system. It also has a Great Red Spot, which is a massive storm larger than Earth.

Page 16 – Day 4

1. F
2. D
3. B
4. J
5. E
6. H
7. G
8. A
9. C
10. I

Page 17 – Day 5

Example response: If I had to plan a mission to another planet, I would choose Mars. Mars is closer to Earth compared to other planets, making the trip shorter and easier for astronauts. It has a solid surface, unlike gas giants like Jupiter, which makes it easier to land and explore. Mars also has water in the form of ice, which is essential for drinking, growing food, and making oxygen, allowing astronauts to stay longer.

Week Two

Moon Phases

Page 22 – Day 1

1. B
2. C
3. B
4. A
5. False. A waxing Moon appears to be getting larger.
6. First Quarter
7. We can't see a New Moon because it is positioned between the Earth and the Sun, so the side of the Moon that is illuminated is facing away from us.

Page 23 – Day 2

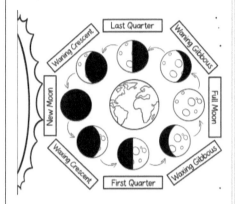

View page 100 for a larger image.

Page 24 – Day 3

1. Full Moon 2. New Moon 3. First quarter

4. Waxing Gibbous 5. Waning Crescent 6. Last Quarter

7. Waxing Crescent 8. Waning Gibbous

9. B) Waning
10. A) Waxing

Page 25 – Day 4

1. H
2. C
3. I
4. A
5. F
6. D
7. E
8. B
9. G

Answer Keys

Page 26 – Day 5

1. Example Response: If you observe a full moon tonight, the moon will be in its last quarter phase about a week later. This is because the moon takes about 29.5 days to complete its cycle of phases, and it moves through each major phase (new moon, first quarter, full moon, and last quarter) roughly every seven days. So, in one week, the moon will have moved to the position where half of it is illuminated, known as the last quarter phase.

2. Example Response: If you were standing on the Moon looking at Earth, you would see the Earth go through phases just like the Moon does from Earth, but in reverse. When people on Earth see a full moon, you would see a "new Earth" (completely dark), and when people on Earth see a new moon, you would see a "full Earth" (completely bright). The Earth's phases would be the opposite of the Moon's phases seen from Earth.

Week Three

Solar & Lunar Eclipses

Page 34 – Day 1

1. B
2. D
3. A
4. C
5. Example response: It is safe to view a lunar eclipse without special glasses because the Moon is not bright enough to damage your eyes. However, during a solar eclipse, the Sun's rays are powerful and can burn your retinas, leading to permanent vison loss.

6. Example response: Ancient people were scared of eclipses because they did not understand what was happening. They might have though it was a negative sign from the gods or that something magical or dangerous was about to happen.

Page 35 – Day 2

1. Sun
2. Moon
3. Penumbra
4. Umbra
5. Earth
6. Moon's orbit
7. Example response: During a solar eclipse, the Moon moves between the Earth and the Sun, blocking out the Sun's light. This creates two types of shadows on Earth: the umbra, where the Sun is completely covered and people see a total eclipse, and the penumbra, where only part of the Sun is blocked and people see a partial eclipse. The diagram shows how the Moon's shadow travels across Earth, making it dark for a little while.

Page 36 – Day 3

1. Solar
2. Lunar
3. Solar
4. Solar
5. Lunar
6. Lunar
7. Lunar
8. Solar
9. Lunar
10. Solar

Page 37 – Day 4

1. G
2. B
3. E
4. J
5. A
6. H
7. C
8. F
9. D
10. I

Page 38 – Day 5

Example response: A total solar eclipse and a total lunar eclipse look different but have some things in common. During a total solar eclipse, the sky gets dark in the daytime because the Moon covers the Sun. You can see a bright ring around the dark Sun, called the corona. During a total lunar eclipse, the Earth's shadow covers the Moon, making it turn a reddish color, sometimes called a "blood moon." Solar eclipses happen during the day, and lunar eclipses happen at night. Both types of eclipses show how the Sun, Earth, and Moon line up and create amazing sights in the sky.

Week Four

Life Cycle of Stars

Page 42 – Day 1

1. D
2. B
3. C
4. A
5. Massive stars go through a life cycle that includes becoming a red supergiant and ending in a supernova explosion, which can leave behind a neutron star or a black hole. Average stars, like our Sun, go through phases including a red giant and end as a white dwarf after shedding their outer layers as a planetary nebula.

Answer Keys

Page 43 - Day 2

PROTOSTAR	RED SUPERGIANT	NEUTRON STAR OR BLACK HOLE
2	4	6

SUPERNOVA	STELLAR NEBULA	MAIN SEQUENCE STAR
5	1	3

Page 44 - Day 3

Example responses:
1. (already written for you) I'm a stellar Nebula, and I'm where stars are born!
2. I'm starting to take shape! I'm a baby star now!
3. (already written for you) I'm a main sequence star, just like the Sun! I'll stay like this for billions of years!
4. I'm getting old and expanding! I'm a Red Giant now!
5. Time to shed my outer layers and form a beautiful planetary nebula!
6. I'm a white dwarf, slowly cooling down for the rest of time.

Page 45 - Day 4

1. J
2. D
3. B
4. G
5. F
6. K
7. H
8. A
9. L
10. E
11. I
12. C

Page 46 - Day 5

Example Response:

Dear Friend,

I hope you are doing well! I want to tell you about what happens to a star like our Sun as it gets older and turns into a red giant. When a star like the Sun runs out of the hydrogen fuel it uses to shine, it starts to change. The star's core gets hotter and the outer layers expand a lot, turning the star into a red giant. This makes the star much bigger and brighter, but also cooler on the surface, which is why it looks red. As the Sun becomes a red giant, the inner planets, like Mercury and Venus, will get so hot that they might be destroyed. Earth will also get very hot, causing the oceans to dry up and the air to disappear. This means that plants, animals, and people wouldn't be able to live there anymore. Studying the life cycle of stars is really important because it helps us understand how stars change over time and how they affect the planets around them. It also teaches us about the creation of new elements and how the universe has evolved. By learning about stars, we can better understand our own Sun and what might happen in the future.

Your friend,
Juliana

Week Five

Constellations

Page 49 - Day 1

1. B
2. A
3. D
4. C
5. B
6. True
7. A
8. C

Page 50 - Day 2

Answers will vary.

Page 53 - Day 3

1. Pegasus
2. Ursa Major
3. Andromeda
4. Canis Major
5. Draco
6. Hercules
7. Cassiopeia
8. Perseus
9. Orion
10. Cygnus

Page 54 - Day 4

1. E
2. C
3. A
4. D
5. F
6. B
7. The swan
8. The captive princess
9. The winged horse

Page 55 - Day 5

Example Response:
Different cultures have different names and stories for the same constellations because they see the stars in ways that match their own beliefs and traditions. People in different parts of the world created their own stories about the night sky based on what was important to them. This shows that the night sky is like a big picture that everyone can look at, but each culture paints it in a different way. Even though we all see the same stars, the meanings we give them can be very different depending on where we come from. This tells us that people are very creative and use the stars to explain the world in a way that makes sense to them.

Answer Keys

Page 60 - Day 1

1. B
2. A
3. D
4. C
5. Example response: No, I've never seen a meteor shower, but I would really like to! I think it would be amazing to watch lots of 'shooting stars' all at once. I've heard that they light up the sky and can be really bright. I think people find meteor showers fascinating because they are rare and it feels special to see so many meteors all at once. It's like a big, natural fireworks show in the sky!

Page 61 - Day 2

		COMET	METEOR	ASTEROID
1.	known for having a bright, glowing tail that can be seen from Earth	✓		
2.	a small, rocky body that orbits the sun, often found in a belt between Mars and Jupiter			✓
3.	often called a "shooting star" when it burns up in Earth's atmosphere		✓	
4.	If this object reaches Earth's surface without burning up, it is called a meteorite.		✓	
5.	this can be as small as a pebble and can also be hundreds of miles wide			✓
6.	mostly made of ice, dust, and rocks	✓		
7.	can be seen as a streak of light in the night sky when it burns up in the atmosphere		✓	
8.	Develops a coma as it nears the Sun	✓		

Page 62 & 63- Day 3

1. Comets
2. Coma
3. Away
4. Meteorite
5. Asteroid
6. Orbit
7. Dust
8. Meteors
9. Shower
10. history

C	E	C	A	D	U	E	N	E	C	O	M	A	T
A	S	E	P	S	O	P	E	I	T	I	M	S	G
M	H	A	B	D	T	U	M	A	S	I	N	B	
O	O	W	D	C	M	T	E	O	R	S	L	E	
U	W	L	M	A	C	S	R	O	N	E	R	G	H
F	E	A	S	R	P	O	Y	O	I	C	A	L	A
L	R	O	Y	S	R	T	M	R	I	I	T	N	V
A	I	S	P	Y	E	O	E	E	T	D	I	S	I
H	O	R	A	M	D	L	T	T	T	O	O	F	O
E	I	W	E	E	A	B	E	E	I	S	N	S	R
Y	A	S	E	R	T	I	O	O	R	O	F	I	T
D	S	B	T	Y	O	V	R	U	Z	Z	N	I	L
U	H	I	B	O	R	N	I	T	I	O	B	Q	N
S	R	A	V	F	R	Y	T	U	V	R	G	Z	L
T	H	O	J	E	R	Y	E	N	O	A	D	F	R
E	H	K	L	I	U	O	F	X	L	O	B	Y	I

View page 100 for a larger image.

Page 64 - Day 4

1. E
2. C
3. A
4. G
5. J
6. B
7. H
8. F
9. I
10. D

Page 65 - Day 5

Example Response:
Dear Friend,
I learned some cool stuff in science class about asteroids, meteors, and comets, and I wanted to share it with you! They're all space rocks, but they're actually pretty different from each other. First, asteroids are big rocks that orbit the sun, kind of like mini planets. Most of them hang out in a place called the Asteroid Belt, which is between Mars and Jupiter. Some are small, like the size of a car, but others are huge, even bigger than a city! Next, there are meteors. A meteor is what you see when a small rock, called a meteoroid, enters Earth's atmosphere and burns up. It's that bright streak of light in the sky that people call a "shooting star," even though it's not a star at all! If a meteor doesn't burn up completely and actually hits the ground, then it's called a meteorite. Finally, there are comets. Comets are like dirty snowballs made of ice, dust, and rock. They travel around the sun in really long orbits. When a comet gets close to the sun, the heat makes the ice turn into gas, creating a glowing tail that can be millions of miles long! That's what makes comets so cool to watch.
Your friend,
Amir

Page 69 - Day 1

1. B
2. C
3. A
4. D
5. Gravity is important in the solar system because it keeps the planets in orbit around the sun. The sun's gravity pulls the planets towards it, preventing them from flying off into space.

Answer Keys

Page 70 – Day 2

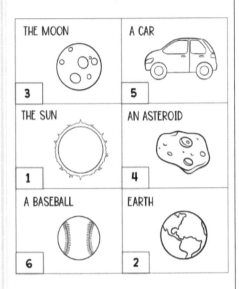

THE MOON **3**	A CAR **5**
THE SUN **1**	AN ASTEROID **4**
A BASEBALL **6**	EARTH **2**

Page 71 – Day 3

1. False
2. True
3. True
4. False
5. True
6. False
7. False
8. True
9. False
10. True

Page 72 – Day 4

1. F
2. B
3. H
4. A
5. C
6. E
7. J
8. D
9. I
10. G

Page 73 – Day 5

1. If Earth's gravity suddenly became weaker, everything would feel a lot lighter. We would be able to jump much higher and maybe even float a little when we walk. It might be fun at first, like being on a trampoline all the time, but it could also be strange and difficult to get used to. Sports and games would be different because the ball would fly higher and farther. Buildings and other tall structures might need to be made stronger to stay standing. Even simple things like pouring water or holding objects might change because gravity wouldn't pull them down as much.

2. When we throw a ball into the air, gravity slows it down as it rises, eventually stopping it and pulling it back down to the ground. Without gravity, the ball would keep moving in the direction we threw it and wouldn't come back down, because there would be no force to pull it back to Earth.

Week Eight

Earth's Rotation and Revolution

Page 77 – Day 1

1. B
2. A
3. B
4. D
5. Example response: Rotation is when Earth spins like a top on its axis. It's like if you spun a basketball on your finger. This spinning is why we have day and night. When your part of Earth is facing the Sun, it's daytime, and when it's turned away, it's nighttime. Earth takes about 24 hours to make one full spin.

Revolution is when Earth travels in a big circle around the Sun. Imagine you're running around a track—Earth is doing something like that around the Sun. This trip around the Sun takes a whole year, or about 365 days, and it's why we have seasons.

Page 78 – Day 2

1. True
2. False
3. True
4. True
5. False
6. True
7. False
8. False
9. False
10. True

Page 79 – Day 3

1. Day
2. Year
3. Revolution
4. Night
5. Orbit
6. Sun
7. Rotation
8. Seasons
9. Axis
10. Tilt

Answer Keys

Page 80 - Day 4

1. F
2. C
3. H
4. A
5. E
6. G
7. I
8. D
9. B

Page 81 - Day 5

1. Example response: If Earth didn't spin, one side would always be day and the other side would always be night. The sunny side would be really hot, and the dark side would be very cold. This would make it hard for plants and animals to live because there would be no day and night changes.

2. Example response: If I could design a planet with a unique rotation and orbit, I would make it spin very slowly so that each side experiences a long day followed by a long night. The planet's orbit would be highly elliptical, bringing it much closer to its star at some points and much farther away at others. This would cause dramatic changes in temperature and create extreme seasons with very hot summers and very cold winters. The long days and nights would lead to unique patterns of life and interesting weather, making the planet a fascinating place with diverse climates and environments.

Week Nine

History of Space Exploration

Page 86 - Day 1

1. B
2. D
3. A
4. C
5. C
6. A
7. B
8. C

Page 87 & 88 - Day 2

Answers will vary.

Page 89- Day 3

1. E
2. C
3. A
4. G
5. J
6. D
7. F
8. I
9. B
10. H

Page 90- Day 4

View page 101 for a larger image.

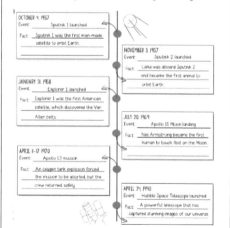

Page 91- Day 5

1. The most significant space exploration event could be the Apollo 11 Moon landing. This event is important because it was the first time humans walked on the Moon. It showed that we could travel to another world and come back safely. The success of Apollo 11 also inspired more exploration and helped us learn a lot about space.

2. The future of space exploration might include sending humans to Mars, building bases on the Moon, and exploring distant planets and moons with advanced robots. We might also find new ways to travel faster in space and discover more about other planets, possibly even finding signs of life beyond Earth.

Moon Phases

Page 23 – Day 2

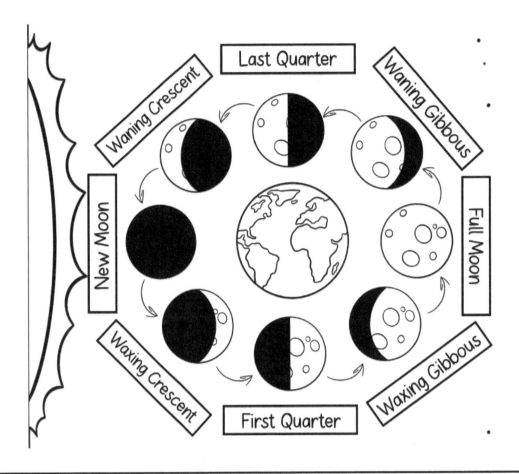

Page 63 – Day 3

Comets, Meteors, and Asteroids

C	E	C	A	D	U	E	N	E	C	O	M	A	T
A	S	E	P	S	O	P	E	I	T	I	M	S	G
M	H	A	B	D	T	U	M	A	S	I	I	N	B
O	O	W	D	C	M	E	T	E	O	R	S	L	E
U	W	L	M	A	C	S	R	O	N	E	R	G	H
F	E	A	S	R	P	O	Y	O	I	C	A	L	A
L	R	O	Y	S	R	T	M	R	I	I	T	N	V
A	I	S	P	Y	E	O	E	E	T	D	I	S	I
H	O	R	A	M	D	L	T	T	T	O	O	F	O
E	I	W	E	E	A	B	E	E	I	S	N	S	R
Y	A	S	E	R	T	I	O	O	R	O	F	I	T
D	S	B	T	Y	O	V	R	U	Z	Z	N	I	L
U	H	I	B	O	R	N	I	T	I	O	B	Q	N
S	R	A	V	F	R	Y	T	U	V	R	G	Z	L
T	H	O	J	E	R	Y	E	N	O	A	D	F	R
E	H	K	L	I	U	O	F	X	L	O	B	Y	I

History of Space Exploration

Page 90 — Day 4

OCTOBER 4, 1957

Event: ___Sputnik 1 launched___

Fact: ___Sputnik 1 was the first man-made___
___satellite to orbit Earth.___

NOVEMBER 3, 1957

Event: ___Sputnik 2 launched___

Fact: ___Laika was aboard Sputnik 2___
___and became the first animal to___
___orbit Earth.___

JANUARY 31, 1958

Event: ___Explorer 1 launched___

Fact: ___Explorer 1 was the first American___
___satellite, which discovered the Van___
___Allen belts.___

JULY 20, 1969

Event: ___Apollo 11 Moon landing___

Fact: ___Neil Armstrong became the first___
___human to touch foot on the Moon.___

APRIL 11-17, 1970

Event: ___Apollo 13 mission___

Fact: ___An oxygen tank explosion forced___
___the mission to be aborted, but the___
___crew returned safely.___

APRIL 24, 1990

Event: ___Hubble Space Telescope launched___

Fact: ___A powerful telescope that has___
___captured stunning images of our universe.___

Looking for more science resources to supplement your child's learning?

Our 'Science Throughout the Year' unit is designed to complement your child's daily science workbook plus additional topics. It provides over 1000 pages and slides of interactive activities, editable PowerPoint slides, lessons, posters, etc. (ALL DIGITAL). Nothing will be mailed to you. You would receive a zip file with all of the editable PowerPoint slides, PDFs, and links to Google Slides.

Reinforce key concepts throughout the year. Simply scan the QR code below to access the unit and enhance your child's science education.

What teachers are saying:

★★★★★

This resource helped me build confidence to teach science! I've always felt very intimidated and overwhelmed. These resources were so engaging! These made teaching science fun for me, which translated to engagement for my kids! I cannot say thank you enough!

- THE TRAVELING TEXAN TEACHER

★★★★★

I love this resource! The slides are beautiful and full of information. It is very well organized, the activities are engaging! The children loved all of the activities. I don't know if it had to do anything with this resource but, my students scored so much better on the FCAT than previous classes. Thank you!

- JOANN SO.

★★★★★

This was one of my best investments this year! My students loved the material and it helped make lesson planning much easier!

-SAMANTHA H.

Contact the Author:
Fatema@thediscoveryapple.com
Contact the Illustrator:
Themagicalgallery@outlook.com

Other workbooks you will love:

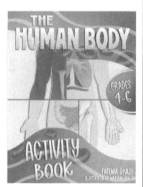

Want Access to my FREE Resource Library?

All in one Place!

Thank You!

Thank you for purchasing this workbook! As a Texas-certified teacher with a Bachelors Degree in Education, and a curriculum designer with over 8 years of experience, I wanted to provide a valuable learning tool for parents and educators like you. I hope you find it beneficial and that it enhances your child's learning experience.

Share Your Thoughts

Your feedback is very important! If you have a moment, please leave a review of this workbook on Amazon. Your honest opinion helps other people discover my work. Thank you for your support!

Warm regards,
Fatema Ghazi

Made in United States
Troutdale, OR
09/20/2024

22982815R00060